poisonous heart

USA TODAY BESTSELLING AUTHOR
PERSEPHONE AUTUMN

BETWEEN WORDS PUBLISHING LLC

Poisonous Heart

Copyright © 2023 by Persephone Autumn and Between Words Publishing LLC

www.persephoneautumn.com

All rights reserved.

No part of this book may be reproduced in any form or by any electronic or mechanical means, including photocopying, information storage and retrieval systems, without written permission from the author except for the use of brief quotations in a book review.

This book is a work of fiction. Names, characters, establishments, organizations, and incidents are either products of the author's imagination or are used fictitiously to give a sense of authenticity. Any resemblance to actual events, places, or persons, living or dead, is entirely coincidental.

If you're reading this book and did not purchase it, or it was not purchased for your use only, or it was purchased on a site I do not advertise I sell on, then it was pirated illegally. Please purchase a copy of your own on a platform where the author advertises she distributes and respect the hard work of this author.

ISBN: 978-1-951477-67-7 (Ebook)

ISBN: 978-1-951477-68-4 (Paperback)

Editor: Ellie McLove | My Brother's Editor

Cover Design: Persephone Autumn | Between Words Publishing LLC

BOOKS BY PERSEPHONE AUTUMN

Lake Lavender Series

Depths Awakened

One Night Forsaken

Every Thought Taken

Devotion Series

Distorted Devotion

Undying Devotion

Beloved Devotion

Darkest Devotion

Sweetest Devotion

Bay Area Duet Series

Click Duet

Through the Lens

Time Exposure

Inked Duet

Fine Line

Love Buzz

Insomniac Duet

Restless Night

A Love So Bright

<u>Artist Duet</u>

Blank Canvas

Abstract Passion

<u>Novellas</u>

Reese

Penny

<u>Stone Bay Series</u>

Broken Sky—Prequel

<u>Standalone Romance Novels</u>

Sweet Tooth

Transcendental

<u>Poetry Collections</u>

Ink Veins

Broken Metronome

Slipping From Existence

Poisonous Heart

Beneath Wildflowers

PUBLISHED UNDER P. AUTUMN

<u>Standalone Non-Romance Novels</u>

By Dawn

*For every person who has had or still struggles with toxic people in their life.
Detoxing from them is the hardest task bestowed upon you, but you are allowed to set them free. You are allowed to move on, without them, and be happy.*

poisonous heart

It is all such a
blur
The way each of you
poisoned my heart.

Each one of you
scarred my soul
in irreversible ways.
Always taking
depleting
sucking me dry
and never satisfied with your fill.

Years ago, I was too
young
naïve
blind to see
all the ways you poisoned my heart.

It took one step
then another
and countless more
until I saw each of you.
Witnessed your true form.
Saw the wickedness in your eyes.
Heard the venom in your words.
Felt the impact on my soul.

You are not solely to blame.
I waited too long to
straighten my spine
use my voice
walk away.

And now that I know
the brand of your poison,
I will never let such toxicity
mar my heart again.

So, thank you.
For teaching me
what evil
tastes, feels like
so I never experience it again.

wrong kind of love

It started when I was young,
learning about the wrong kind of love
or at least,
what I thought was love.

The toxic delusion full of
sadness
hurt
suffering

Little did I know
this behavior
formed a mold
shaded my perception
showed me all the wrong ways
to love.

It's still there

whispering in my thoughts
trickling through my veins
filtering through my marrow

The wrong kind of love.

But it's the only
love
I will ever know.

cursed

Have you ever thought...
Am I cursed?

As the years
tick by
I ask myself this
more often than not.

Am I cursed?

Cursed to feel
pain
hurt
heartache
agony

Cursed to be surrounded by

the same cycle of
people
symptoms
anguish

Made to feel
small
unimportant
annoying
out of place

Once upon a time
I thought I broke
the cycle.
Thought I broke
free
from the weight pulling me
down
down
down

But the reminders
cycle back

The reminders tell me
the cycle will never
break.
You will never
be free.

The reminders tell me to

sit down
shut up
go about life
and plaster on my
fake smile.

first taste

I was young
when I got my
first taste of
poison

Drip fed
Little by little

Small doses that
made poison seem
normal
typical
something everyone consumed.

When you're fed poison
in heart-shaped packages
coated in words like
love

family
blood,
you feel wrong
saying no
telling them to stop
to be kind
to show true affection
to accept you.

That's the thing about
the first taste of poison.
It goes down harshly
with claws
and pain
and agony.

But over time, poison becomes
smoother
familiar
tolerable
acceptable

I don't remember
the very first taste.
But that's how poison works.

first glimpse

Poison is an
unending cycle.

Dose
weaken
wound
blanket with lies
false smiles
artificial affection
repeat.

My first glimpse of
poison
was under the guise of
love.

At the time,
I was oblivious to

poison.

Before my legs knew
strength,
before I could stand tall,
poison already ran
through my veins.

Before I'd spoken my
first words,
poison
contaminated my soul.

She said it was
love
as she spat words of
hate.
She said it was
okay
as she took
hit after hit of "love"
in the form of
fists
powder
dark liquid.

My first glimpse of
poison
came early in life.
I did not understand,
could not comprehend,

how each dose would
impact me.

But, oh
How every drop of
poison
molded my future.

the shape of poison

You may not know this,
but poison has a shape.

Those unaffected by
poison
picture it as
liquid
a tincture
something slipped into food.

But poison,
true poison,
has
a face
a name
a beating, black heart.

Real poison is

familiar
a smiling face
an artificial embrace
whispered lies
and the unending
drip
drip
drip
of toxicity.

Though poison comes in many forms,
genuine poison is
someone close
that spreads their venom like
cancer
with one intention.

Death
of your light
of your heart
of your soul
of you.

how poison works

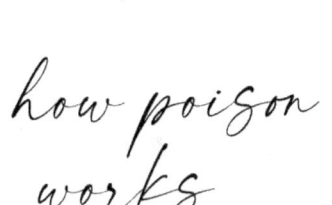

Warped,
my perspective.
Reclusive,
my thoughts.
Unworthy,
my soul.
Tainted,
my heart.

This is how poison
works
consumes
smears
shreds
eats
corrupts

Before I understood

worth
beauty
kindness
Poison robbed me of them.

Poison taught me I was
never good enough
a pedophiles wet dream
weak and spineless.

Poison painted the world in
red and
black and
shadows and
doom

And before I had the
opportunity
to think for myself,
poison
sunk its claws
in my mind
in my heart
in my soul
with the promise to
never let go.

You see,
that is how poison works.
It blinds you to
goodness

joy
peace
truth

And after decades of poison,
it's finally time to
detox

when poison blames you

Poison has the
power
caliber
audacity
to spin the narrative
to twist the knife deeper
to make you believe
you are to blame.

Every step forward,
every truth questioned,
every opportunity at something good,
poison stomped
down
down
down

When perfection wasn't achieved,

poison stood at the podium,
voice thick with blame.
When standards were met with resistance,
poison stood tall and pointed a blameful finger.
When shadows fall over life,
when you want it all to
stop
end
cease to exist
poison squares its shoulders and says, "Not strong enough."

That's the thing about
poison...
it plays the victim,
pins you with guilt
and shame
and pain.
Poison blames you until you
relent
believe
forfeit
crumble

Poison only cares about one thing,
and it isn't you.

first detox

I remember my
first detox
from poison.

Early in life,
I got a lethal dose of
poison.
A dose strong enough to
leech my blood
blacken my heart
steal my soul
corrupt my future

In the days that followed,
I went through my
first detox.

But my mind was too

young
frazzled
distraught
to realize I was in detox.

And my heart was too
focused
excited
light
at the idea of young love.

Soon, though
that first detox came to an end.
And the cycle of
poison
started once more.

promiscuity poison

Whore was never a title
I wore over my breast
like a business owner.

But poison warped my view on
love
affection
attention
sex

Desperate for an ounce of
love
attention
I toed the line of
relationships not mine.

Promiscuous, but not a whore.

My lips touched those that
did not belong to me.
My fingers explored skin that
did not belong to me.
My heart craved attention from people that
did not belong to me.

Meaningless sex to
break the cherry
feel desirable
have eyes on me
even if only for a breath.

Whore had never been my title,
but I wore a red A nonetheless.
Always faithful in relationships,
but willing to be the
mistress
secret
slut on the side
for others.

This was my brand of
poison.
This was just another way
poison stole a piece of my soul.

poison's disguise

To escape the arms of
poison,
I dove headfirst into the
unknown
first opportunity
unsavory situations

Little did I know,
I left one brand of
poison
for another.

Poison disguised as
freedom
hope
a full breath
an exhilarating life

And because I'd tasted poison before,
I did not shy away from
signs
red flags
reasons to
run
run
run

You see,
poison recognizes poison.
It disguises itself,
paints false pictures of
a more desirable life.
It pretends to
be what you want
deliver what you need
fulfill all your dreams

And though it is a new brand of
poison,
it lies all the same
it breaks you all the same
it cackles with an evil black heart
all the same

In the end,
no matter what face it wears,
poison is one thing...
Poison.

a light in the dark

Trapped by poison
again
I found a glimmer of
light
in the dark

The light was
unexpected
appealing
incentive
a reason to keep
sipping poison

Years of this sparkle
kept me addicted to
poison.
But once the shine began to
fade

darken
be affected by poison too,
the glimmer was no longer
enough

Bathed in poison,
a hint of light can
tempt
lure
pull you in deeper

But the moment that light
fizzles
fades
vanishes from sight,
you get a glimpse of
reality
falsehoods
the lie

You get a glimpse of the
new poison
and how it fed you
worse than any other before

second detox

The second detox from
poison
was different from the first.

I suppose it should be.
No two poisons are the same.

Unlike the first,
my second detox showed promise
a positive outcome
easy relief
from the venom in my veins.

That was
until poison glimpsed my
smile
laughter
light-heartedness

at no longer being under its spell.

And if I'd learned anything over the years,
poison doesn't like
when you're happy
when it can't control you
when you don't bend to its will

So as I detoxed from poison
again
I fought with its
claws in my skin
teeth bared in anger
degrading words in my ears

What poison didn't remember during my second detox...
I'd been fighting all my life
I'd already died and come back
I'd grown and set aside juvenile tendencies

More than that,
I had a reason to fight
harder than ever.

And for that reason,
poison would never win.

when poison gets lonely

When you step back and see
poison
for what it really is,
you actually feel
sorry for it.

Here's the thing about
poison,
without a host to
infect,
poison is a lonely, pathetic soul.

Without someone to
blame
ridicule
show off to
fluff their ego
poison is nothing but a

lifeless shell

And when poison gets
lonely,
poison doubles down
pushes harder
slashes
cuts
digs the knife deeper,
just for a delicious hit of its
toxic aftertaste

One thing that will never change with
poison...
it will always
knock you down
dose you, again and again and again
cut without remorse
rip you to shreds while you beg it to stop

And poison does this
with a smile on its face.

third detox

When poison witnessed my
humor
relief
success
gaiety,
it brought a knife to my jugular

Sharp blade to my throat,
poison spewed harsh words
with its spit-stained lips turned up at the corners

Poison said
hateful
hurtful
irreversible falsehoods
in the hopes of beating me into submission

But after two detoxes from

poison,
I wasn't someone that
bowed easily
believed the lie
yielded under pressure

I was no longer
young
naïve
weak
gullible

My third detox from
poison
was the easiest and most difficult.
Because poison
refused to let me go
refused to let me grow
refused to let me smile
refused to let me live in a world without them

Poison was determined.
But so was I.

Under the oppressive thumb of
poison,
I missed the beauty of
life
love
laughter
the world

And as I slowly got a glimpse of life
without poison,
I gained strength
I gained love
for myself, for others, from others
I gained insight.

Most of all,
without poison,
I learned how to breathe again.

saying goodbye to poison

The funny thing about
poison...
Once you've had a taste,
you recognize it going forward.

Poison never
looks the same
sounds the same
tastes the same

With each new poison,
it takes on a different
face
voice
smell
flavor
And though it disguises itself well,
poison presents itself

with small tells
matching its predecessor.

Poison is pure
temptation,
waiting in the wings
eager and hungry and ready to destroy.

No one is immune to a new dose of
poison,
I fell into its trap
over
and over
and over
and over

But every time I choose to
stand
fight back
say "no more,"
I tell poison
goodbye

poison's intermission

The quiet before the storm,
this is
poison's intermission.

Some would say
silence is absence
bask in the reprieve
let go and move on

And during
poison's intermission
I believed the absence
I basked in the reprieve
I let go
I moved on

For the first time in my life,
I tasted freedom

I felt weightless
I experienced joy

For the first time in my life,
I'd broken free.

Or so I thought.

One key fact about
poison...
it never lets go,
it never moves on,
it only spreads,
intent on infiltrating
until you cave

by force

When you don't feed
poison
what it wants
what it *needs*
poison
takes by force

Unwelcome calls
Insulting messages
Celebratory cards stuffed with
defamatory
cruel
disrespectful
words on lined pages

Poison was angry.
Poison demanded attention.
Poison refused to be denied.

But little did
poison know...
I had the antidote
and poison
would never infect me again

life without poison

Those infected by
poison
fear they will
never experience life
without poison.

This is how
poison
keeps their claws in you.

But a life without
poison
is possible
exists

A life without
poison
takes time

takes effort
takes strength
takes perseverance

Poison will
always try to reinfect
always try to maintain a foothold
always
try
try
try

But once you stand up to
poison
once you say
no more
this is when
you will truly have
a life without poison

This is when you are truly
free

MORE BY PERSEPHONE

Ink Veins

Persephone Autumn's debut poetry collection, Ink Veins, explores topics of depression, love, and self-discovery with a raw, unfiltered voice.

Broken Metronome

When the music of the heart dies...

Broken Metronome is an angsty poetry collection full of heartache and the possibility of what may have been.

Slipping From Existence

Would it be so bad to slip from existence? Would it be so bad to give in to the darkness?

Slipping From Existence is a dark poetry collection centered around depression and coping while maintaining a brave face.

Beneath Wildflowers

You were the sweetest, most precious surprise.

A soul with a tender heart.

I will love and miss you forever.

As you rest beneath the wildflowers.

Depths Awakened

A small town romance which captivates you from the start.

Mags and Geoff are two broken souls who have sworn off love. Vowed to never lose anyone else. But their undeniable attraction brings them together and refuses to let go.

One Night Forsaken

One night. No names. No romance. Just fun. Nothing more—at least, that's what she tells herself. Until he appears in her coffee shop months later with that addictive smile. She swore off commitment. He vows to never love again. But the more they fight it, the more life brings them together.

Every Thought Taken

As young children, an unshakable friendship brought them together. As teens, they discovered an undeniable love. Then life pulled them in different directions—into darkness and light—and slowly ripped them apart. Years later, he returns home in the hopes of a second chance with his first love and to conquer the demons of his past.

Distorted Devotion

Free-spirited Sarah lives life to the fullest. When a new love interest enters her life, she starts receiving strange gifts and letters. She doesn't want to relinquish her freedom or new love, but fears the consequences.

Transcendental

A musician in search of his muse and a woman grieving the loss of her husband. Two weeks at an exclusive retreat and their connection rivals all others. Until she leaves early without notice. But he refuses to give up until he finds her again.

The Click Duet

High school sweethearts torn apart. When fate gives them a second chance, one doesn't trust they won't be hurt again. Through the Lens (Click Duet #1) and Time Exposure (Click Duet #2) is an angsty, second chance, friends to lovers romance with all the feels.

Broken Sky

Their eyes meet across the bar, but she looks away first. Does her best to give him zero attention. But when he crowds her on the dancefloor, she can't deny the instant chemistry. After one night together, he marks her as his. Unfortunately, another woman thinks he belongs to her.

THANK YOU

Thank you so much for reading **Poisonous Heart**. If you wouldn't mind taking a moment to leave a review on the retailer site where you made your purchase, Goodreads and/or BookBub, it would mean the world to me.

Reviews help other readers find and enjoy the book as well.

Much love,
　　Persephone

CONNECT WITH PERSEPHONE

Connect with Persephone
www.persephoneautumn.com

Subscribe to Persephone's newsletter
www.persephoneautumn.com/newsletter

Join Persephone's reader's group
Persephone's Playground

Follow Persephone online

- instagram.com/persephoneautumn
- facebook.com/persephoneautumnwrites
- tiktok.com/@persephoneautumn
- bookbub.com/authors/persephone-autumn
- goodreads.com/persephoneautumn
- amazon.com/author/persephoneautumn
- pinterest.com/persephoneautumn

ACKNOWLEDGMENTS

To my incredible family! Life hasn't always been easy, but through all the shit, you stuck around. You lifted me up in difficult times, hugged me harder and longer, and gave me the confidence to see who and what truly matters. I love you so much and wouldn't be who I am without you.

Ellie at My Brother's Editor! Even my poetry is whack when it hits your inbox. But you always make it shine. Thank you for always having my back and being a badass. Love you!

Bloggers!! I would be nowhere without you! Thank you for reading my words, creating magical edits and videos, and promoting my books all over the internet. YOU ROCK!!

Author peeps... I love you! This business is rough and exhausting, but I love how we lean on and support each other. To belong to a community where every person wants everyone to thrive and succeed... I love it and you!

Readers are the best humans! Thank you to each and every one of you for reading my words. For choosing one of my books, thank you times a million. If I could hug you all, my tentacle arms would squeeze you tight.

ABOUT THE AUTHOR

USA Today Bestselling Author Persephone Autumn lives in Florida with her wife and psycho cat. A proud mom with a cuckoo grandpup. An ethnic food enthusiast who has fun discovering ways to vegan-ize her favorite non-vegan foods. Most days, you'll find her with a tea latte or fruity concoction in her hand. If given the opportunity, she would intentionally get lost in nature.

For years, Persephone did some form of writing; mostly journaling or poetry. After pairing her poetry with images and posting them online, she began the journey of writing her first novel.

She mainly writes romance and poetry, but on occasion dips her toes in other works. Look for her non-romance publications under P. Autumn.

www.ingramcontent.com/pod-product-compliance
Lightning Source LLC
Chambersburg PA
CBHW050335120526
44592CB00014B/2190